THE
DRAG
DICTIONARY

An illustrated glossary of fierce queen slang

ALBA DE ZANET & ROBERTO GARCIA

Hardie Grant

BOOKS

What we serve!

To all the Drag Queens & Kings: our Superheroes

We LOVE you! Why? Because you are a living example of how everybody's edges and corners should be celebrated, all while trying to outshine each other with big hair, brilliant makeup and amazing looks.

You are the essence of positivity not just for yourself but for everyone. Your attitude and enthusiasm are contagious, and we believe that you make the world a brighter and better place.

With this book we want to honour you, our superheroes – all the drag queens, kings and allies around the world who get out there every day and show us how to bring out the best in ourselves.

Thank you!

Alba & Roberto

Attitude

/ˈætəˌtud/

It's all about being legendary!

'Serving attitude' can shape the full characteristic of a queen's presence or performance. To succeed, you not only have to serve couture looks, but also bring more than 100% attitude to your performance or strut down the runway like you own it.

'Her upbeat attitude kept the children gagging for more!'

Pepper LaBeija

7

Back Rolls

/bæk roʊlz/

We are all about body positivity.

'Back rolls' is used to describe the kind of rolls that occur on your back when you are slightly overweight. This well-known read became famous through *RuPaul's Drag Race*. Jade Jolie quipped to Alyssa Edwards that she had fat rolls all over her back. Alyssa's response is probably one of the most famous lines to come out of the *Drag Race* franchise.

'Back roooooooooolls?!'

Beat

/bit/

Don't worry! No one is going to hit you.

'To beat' refers to dabbing powder onto your face. Literally hitting it. A 'beat face' describes an amazing and flawless makeup look. This term is especially used in the beauty industry.

**'Henny, you look busted!
Let me beat your face.'**

Body-ody-ody

/ˈbadi-adi-adi/

This term is used to describe a queen who has a very impressive feminine form and shows off her figure. The 'ody-ody' at the end adds extra emphasis to the term.

'That queen is serving body-ody-ody for days!'

Naomi Smalls

13

Busted

/ˈbʌstɪd/

'Looking busted' describes a queen who is either ugly or sloppily put together. She has an unpolished or messy appearance, e.g. her beard shines through her makeup or her wig is badly adjusted. It is a term used to insult another queen.

'Oh gurl, didn't she have enough time for her makeup? She looks busted!'

Charisma, Uniqueness, Nerve & Talent

/kəˈrɪzmə, juˈnɪknəs, nɜrv ænd ˈtælənt/

These are the four qualities that RuPaul and the judges are looking for in a drag queen on the hit show *RuPaul's Drag Race*. The queen with the biggest C.U.N.T. will likely win and snatch the crown.

'This queen has the full package. She has charisma, uniqueness, nerve and talent.'

Cheesecake

/ˈtʃizˌkeɪk/

There is always time for dessert.

This delicious term describes a queen with not only a gorgeous and curvy body but also the ability to sell her sexiness.

'Look at this cheesecake! Serving all this body, she looks yummy!'

Children

/ˈtʃɪldrən/

This term can refer to drag mothers who take up-and-coming drag queens under their wings as their drag children and teach them valuable drag knowledge.

It can also refer to an audience. This is because they are taking care of the audience by serving looks, reading them or simply giving them a sickening performance.

'The children were living for her performance and tipped her a lot.'

Clock

/klak/

Clock o'what?

'To clock' someone means to expose a hidden side of a person. Usually, it refers to pointing out a person's flaws or to uncovering the truth.

It originates from the word 'clock'. To be more precise, it refers to the face of a clock as a metaphor for the human face.

'No one is gonna clock the fact that I'm not a real woman.'

Willam Belli

Cross-dresser

/krɔs-ˈdrɛsər/

Are they a woman or a man?

'Cross-dressing' is the act of wearing clothes associated with the opposite sex. It's about disguise, comfort and self-expression. 'Cross-dressing' was a common practice in the theatre, during the Renaissance, when men and boys dressed as women and played female roles.

'Thor and Hercules were some of the first cross-dressers, and they already looked stunning in women's clothes.'

Cunty

/kʌnti/

It's gonna get naughty!

The term 'cunty' describes a person's highly offensive or unpleasant mood. 'Cunty' can be used to call out someone for their nasty, arrogant or cocky behaviour. It's a sweeter way of calling someone a c**t. But it can also mean having a fierce feminine attitude.

'Sister, stop acting so cunty! You are being really mean.'

27

Dip/Death Drop

/dɪp/dɛθ drɑp/

Dip? Death drop? Let's explain!

A dip is a dance move that originates from a style of voguing, during which the dancer (depending on the category) gracefully or dramatically falls backwards into a lying pose onto the ground.

Laganja Estranja

The term 'death drop' refers to the same dance move and has been used in *RuPaul's Drag Race* for a long time. It has gained more importance during the course of its history.

Both terms are a matter of passionate discussion in the scene.

'What was that? An earthquake? No, she just did a death drop!'

Drag King/ Drag Queen

/dræg kɪŋ/dræg kwin/

The real royals just arrived!

Drag kings and queens show us that gender is all about performance. They are the ones that led the Stonewall riots and the fight for queer rights.

'This drag king (or drag queen) is a real hero.'

Stormé DeLarverie & Marsha P. Johnson

Duct Tape

/dʌkt teɪp/

It's gonna get sticky.

The uses of duct tape are almost infinite. But, on the drag scene, duct tape is particularly known for pulling back male genitalia to create the illusion of having a flat crotch area.

Drag kings often use duct tape
for binding their breasts to create
a flat chest.

**'She didn't use a lot of duct tape.
She has a meaty tuck.'**

Dusted

/ˈdʌstɪd/

It's all about glitter and sparkles!

'Dusted' is the opposite of 'busted' and describes a queen who appears flawless in her drag transformation. A 'dusted' queen is not only polished and professional in her presence or performance, but also a drag queen to look up to for inspiration.

'I admire pageant queens; they always look dusted!'

Eleganza
Extravaganza

/eleˈgaːntsa ɛkˌstravaˈgaːntsa/

Ready to be blown away?

This is the ultimate showstopping, gag-worthy and breathtaking runway category existing. In this category queens walk and serve looks with incredible amounts of elegance.

'She was serving pure eleganza extravaganza with that dress!'

Manila Luzon

37

Fierce

/fɪrs/

Stunning individuals get over here!

'Fierce' is a very positive and cheering term for exceptionally stylish or impressive drag queens who attract attention. It can also be used to outline an appearance, characteristic or an action.

'Hunty, you are giving me life! You are serving fierce lip-syncs tonight.'

Fishy

/ˈfɪʃi/

You asked for seafood?

'Fishy' queens are highly feminine queens. Today, the term is considered offensive towards trans women and cis women. All body parts are beautiful and none of them defines a person's gender.

'She looks so fishy!'

Gag

/gæg/

Don't forget to breathe!

This term refers to a dramatic, shocked reaction either to a look, performance or even a shady read. 'Gag' can also be used as a single word and shouted out to express satisfaction or surprise.

'Gag on my eleganza!'

43

House Down

/haʊs daʊn/

Can your ceiling hold it?

This term is often used at the end of sentences; it serves as a spoken exclamation point. For extra emphasis, it can be followed by 'boots'.

'All the queens tonight performed the house down boots!'

Hunty

/ˈhʌnti/

Let the hunt begin! Wait, what?

Luckily, this term has nothing to do with traditional hunting. It is a mix of the expressions 'honey' and 'c**t'. Hunty can be used as a pet name for friends or lovers.

'Hunty, do you want to come over, have a kiki and spill some tea?'

47

Judy

/ˈdʒudi/

'Judy' is a way to describe a person you would consider a very good or close friend. The term originates from the gay slang 'friend of Dorothy' – a secret code that gay men used to use to identify each other, dating as far back as World War II. Dorothy in *The Wizard of Oz* was played by Judy Garland, and she has long been celebrated as a gay icon.

'I need to spill the tea to my best Judy right now!'

Kai Kai

/kaɪ kaɪ/

Now we're talking!

'Kai kai' is the sexual interaction between two drag queens. It can also be used for queens hooking up out of drag.

'After a long night of partying, my squirrel friend and I decided to kai kai!'

Kiki

/kiki/

'Kiki' is a social gathering for the purpose of gossiping, small talk or an intimate conversation.

It comes from 'kiking', which is used to describe the sound of laughter. 'Kiki' must never be confused with 'kai kai'.

'Sis, let's have a kiki and sip some tea!'

Library

/ˈlaɪˌbrɛri/

Shhh... queens are reading!

The 'library' is an imaginary place in which drag queens are invited to 'read' or to say shady things about other queens. It refers to the fact that you 'read' in a 'library'.

**'The library is now open.
Let's read this girl for filth!'**

Lip-Sync

/lɪp-sɪŋk/

Let the music play!

'Lip-syncing' is a performance almost every drag performer must know. It's usually the main act in a drag show, where drag queens move their lips to the lyrics of a song without singing for real.

'She is a lip-sync assassin! It looks like she is singing!'

Lypsinka

Mop

/map/

Tidying up with drag queens.

'To mop' something is to use the five-finger discount; in other words, to steal something. Watch out for all the shady queens and thieves.

'I just got mopped – my dress is missing and my wig is gone!'

No Tea, No Shade

/noʊ ti, noʊ ʃeɪd/

A combination of the terms 'to spill the tea' and 'to throw shade'. It is a very common expression meaning 'I don't mean to disrespect you, but...' and then followed by a 'read'. There is an even harsher version of the saying: 'All tea, all shade', which means 'I don't care if it offends you'.

'No tea, no shade, but you need to fix your mug and weave.'

61

Okurr

/ˌoʊˈkɚɪ/

Tongue exercise ahead!

To say this word properly, you just have to say 'okay' with a sassy attitude while trilling the 'r'. The origin of this famous term, which is used by drag queens all over the globe, is still being debated.

'It's very messy in here, kinda like your outfit. Okurr!'

Padding

/ˈpædɪŋ/

Changing your silhouette has never been so easy.

Everyone has different body shapes. By wearing hip padding, for example, you can balance out wide shoulders and change the body shape completely. Padding is made of foam and is a great tool for drag queens and kings to achieve their desired body shape.

'You need to start padding, your butt looks flat.'

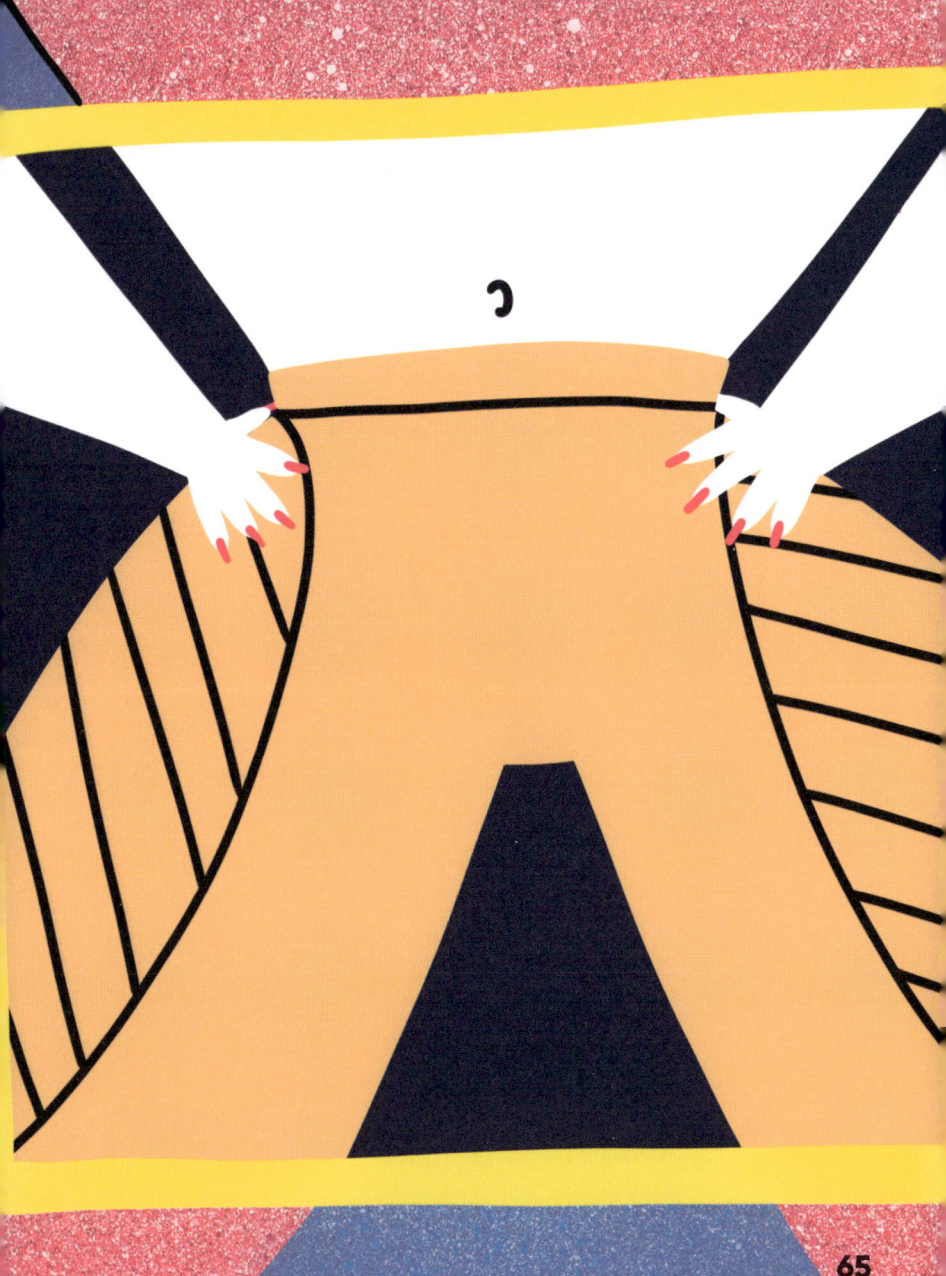

Queen

/kwin/

The description of a female drag artist. The term is also used to honour a beautiful person, who is kind, selfless, caring, determined and brave. A queen fully embraces all that and doesn't let anybody disrespect her fabulosity.

'She entered the room so gallantly. She's such a queen.'

Gene Malin

Reading

/ˈrɛdɪŋ/

Let's go back to school, because reading is what? FUN-damental!

'Reading' is a real art form and means to insult. But you don't insult right away – you wrap it up nicely and cleverly, so that the queen being read has to unpack it.

'Let's close the library! These reads are getting shady.'

Serve

/sɜrv/

Dinner is ready!

'To serve' describes the ability to present oneself in a particular way, giving the audience the ultimate performance and exactly what they want.

'She was serving face and look.'

Shade

/ʃeɪd/

Who is blocking the sun?

In the documentary *Paris is Burning*, Dorian Corey explains that 'shade' comes from 'reading'. 'Throwing shade' is to insult someone very subtly with a nasty backhanded comment; in other words, saying something without really saying it. The act of 'throwing shade' has been in the drag community for years.

'Stop throwing shade; you're getting real cunty!'

Bianca Del Rio

Sickening

/ˈsɪkənɪŋ/

Feeling nauseous, but in a good way.

To look 'sickening' is to look beyond stunning or incredibly breathtaking in appearance or performance.

'I'm gagging; her outfit tonight looks sickening!'

Slay

/sleɪ/

She just murdered the children, but the kids are alright.

In drag lingo the term 'slay' has a different definition. Shouting 'slay' out loud is like praising a queen for her performance or sickening look. 'Slaying' on stage simply means delivering an amazing show.

'Look at her strut! She is slaying the runway. All eyes are on her!'

Yvie Oddly

Squirrel Friends

/ˈskwərəl frɛndz/

Protect your nuts!

'Squirrel friends' derives from 'girlfriends'. It refers to drag queens, especially those who hide their 'nuts' – their genitalia – by tucking them backwards between their legs to simulate the look of female private parts.

'Let's spill some tea between us squirrel friends.'

Tea

/ti/

Do you want some sugar with it?

'Tea' or 'T' refers to the truth in terms of gossip, information or true facts. It derives from 'tea-room', which is another name for public restrooms where men secretly met for sexual encounters. 'Spilling the tea' means making someone else's secrets public.

'Hunty, it's time to spill the T!'

Tongue Pop

/tʌŋ pɒp/

Sometimes you don't need words to throw some shade.

A 'tongue pop' is a noise made with the mouth, lips and tongue. It is usually put at the end of a witty comment to emphasise it or as a sassy response. The facial expression is also very relevant. It was popularised by the drag queen Alyssa Edwards.

'You look sickening tonight!'
tongue pop

Alyssa Edwards

Tuck

/tʌk/

Ouuch! That's gonna hurt!

'Tucking' refers to the practice of putting genitalia between and behind the legs, so that it's invisible from the front of the body. To create the highly feminine body fantasy, drag queens use duct tape or tight underwear. A 'meaty tuck' is a poorly executed 'tuck', which is large or bulging.

'Tuck it tight, so nobody can clock the fact that you're a man!'

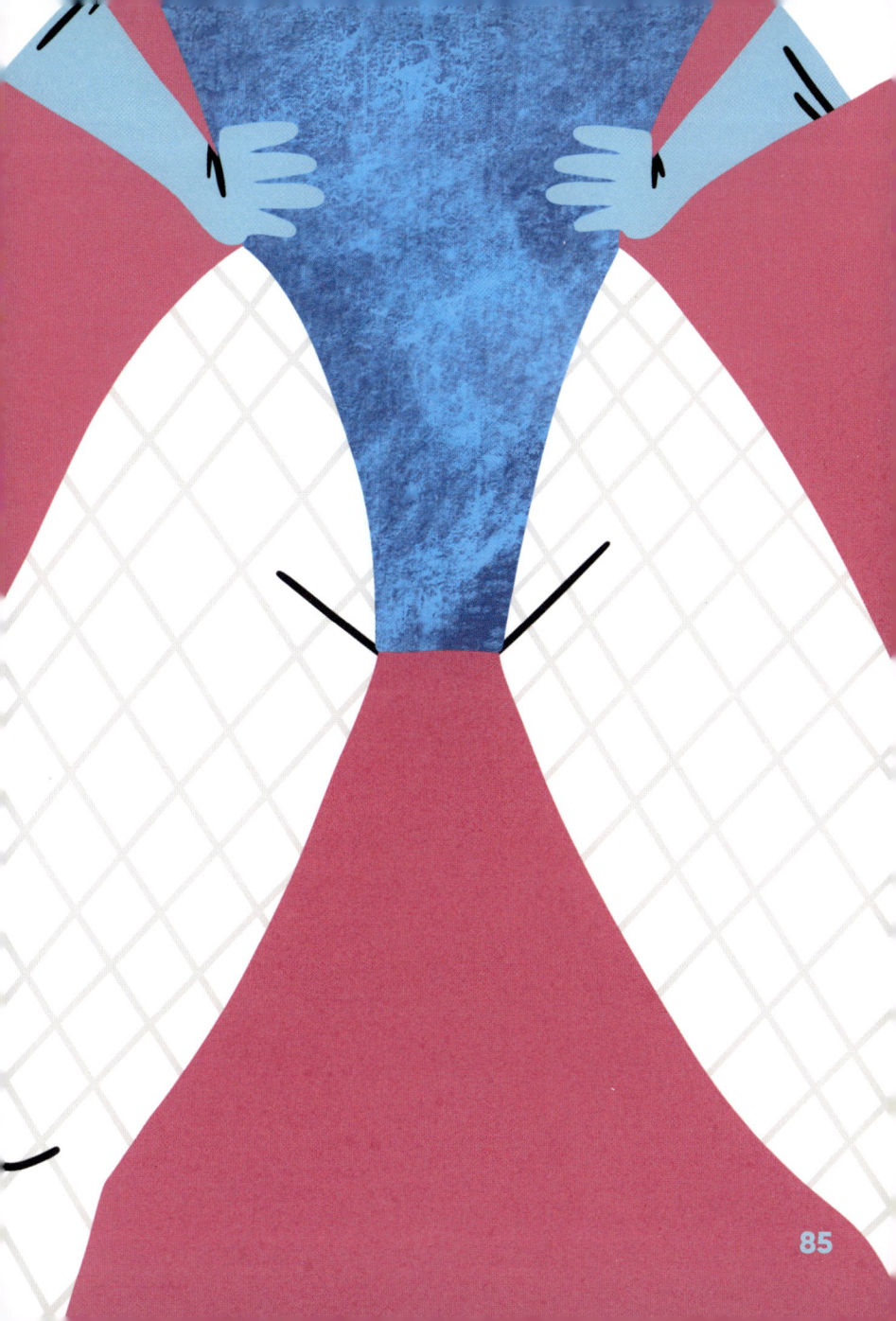

Vogue

/voʊg/

A dance style which originated in the late 1980s from the ballroom scene. The dance imitates the poses found in *Vogue* magazine, which is where the term derives from. It became famous in 1990 through Madonna's song *Vogue* and the documentary *Paris is Burning*. This dance is now a phenomenon all around the world.

'She is voguing the house down. Duckwalking, serving face, spinning and dipping.'

Willi Ninja

Werk

/wɜrk/

No time card needed!

This is probably one of the most used words in the world of drag queens. The term is used to hype up a performer and show them a lot of love because they are slaying the stage.

'She made us all gag for days! WEEEEEERK!'

Wig Reveal

/wɪg rɪˈviːl/

Keep it on if nothing is going to be revealed.

The term simply describes pulling off the wig and revealing another one beneath it. Sometimes also to perform an unexpected act.

Wig reveals have gained more and more popularity in shows and have become a real trend.

'She did two wig reveals, and every wig underneath was sickening.'

Sasha Velour

Yas

/jaz/

An expression of great pleasure, excitement or encouragement, which is taken from the word 'yes'. It originated with queer people of colour in the late 1980s, specifically those involved in ballroom culture. 'Yas' is often yelled when drag queens or voguers perform to cheer them on.

'Yaaas queen! You're slaying this house down!'

Paris Dupree

10s across the board

/tɛnz əˈkrɔs ðə bɔrd/

Maths is important to be a fierce queen.

This perfect score is sought for in judged competitions, like beauty pageants. It was popularised in the 1980s NYC ballroom scene.

'She definitely won the vogue battle and deserved all 10s across the board!'

Types of Queen

Every drag queen is unique.

New styles and art forms are being born daily. But here we go with the most common drag queen styles of today.

Yas sisters!

Activessle

This special type of drag queen often comes in groups. They combine the art of drag with religious symbolism for activism, calling attention to certain issues. The most famous group are 'The Sisters of Perpetual Indulgence'.

Bearded

The term already says it: a drag queen that has facial hair. The beard is an element of the finished look. They often want to achieve confusion. It's a sub-category of genderfuck.

Bio/Faux/AFAB

This queen was born as a female. They apply the art of traditional feminine drag to themselves to achieve an over-the-top female impersonator look.

Butch

A drag queen who is masculine, often used to refer to gay men doing drag for the first time.

Camp

Based on clown styling, this queen likes bold, colourful eye makeup and fashion. Most of these queens perform comedy.

Club

A queen style resulting from the 1980s/1990s NYC club kid scene. They wear artistic fashion along with unique and bold makeup.

Genderfuck

This queen uses a mix of masculine and feminine characteristics to create her own style, including her attitude and lifestyle.

Goth

A drag queen who likes to be scary and dark. She takes her inspiration from gothic and horror movies. They rarely put on colourful makeup.

Pageant

A pageant queen is an extremely polished and feminine version of a drag queen. They mostly compete in beauty contests.

Transdrag

A transdrag queen is a queen who has started transitioning into the opposite gender.

Drag Family

Family

Drag families, also known as 'houses', have an essential role in the ballroom scene. As queer people, most drag performers get to choose their family or create their own house. A house is a safe place and usually a replacement for a real family, and a community in which queer people can live together.

Mother

Drag mothers are the ones who introduce queens into the world of drag by putting on their first wig and showing them how to walk in heels. They act as a mentor, give tips and help out when needed. Like a real mother, they run the house, set the rules and try to bring harmony into the family.

Daughter

From the first time someone is put in drag by another drag queen, they become related and become daughter and mother. An 'adopted' drag queen often takes the last name of her drag mother to pay tribute to her.

More Glossy Glossary

Baking/Cooking

A makeup technique that involves applying a lot of powder over the foundation and letting it set, while your own body heat melts the makeup into the skin.

Bar queen

Usually a term to describe a drag queen that only performs in small bars. It's considered an insult.

Binding

The process of taping breasts or wearing a binder. Some drag kings adopt this technique to create a male illusion.

Booger

Another term for a 'busted' drag queen. Used not only for bad makeup and hair, but also for bad clothing.

Bubble gum

A term to describe a little accident while being tucked. It's when the scrotum skin starts sliding under the tape and looks like chewed up bubble gum.

Cakes

Simply a description for butt cheeks. 'Serving cake' means to show off the butt.

Category
This term comes from the ballroom scene. Contestants walk, perform and compete with each other based on different skills and themes.

Chop
Another word coming from the ballroom scene, which refers to the contestant being eliminated or disqualified and not continuing in the competition.

Come through!
An expression which means 'to do extremely well' or 'slay'. It is also used for cheering.

Condragulations!
The drag version of congratulations.

Feel one's oats
To feel energetic and more animated.

Five o'clock shadow
This term describes the beard that is already shining through the makeup on a drag queen's face. It's considered a read.

Flippers
An expression for false teeth. Pageant queens wear flippers so they don't show any gaps or crooked teeth when they smile.

For the gods
A saying meaning that something or someone is perfect.

Garage doors
Using only one single eyeshadow colour on the eyelids.

Herstory
A mix of the words 'history' and 'her'. The 'his' is replaced to create a feminine version of the word.

Hog body
A description for a queen who doesn't have the kind of feminine figure often achieved by cinching with a corset.

Let them have it
Serving stunning drag and impressing people.

Mug
Another word for a drag queen's face.

Out of the bag
An expression for a cheap wig with no styling.

Paint
To put on makeup.

Peanut butter
A wordplay for things that are spreadable and delicious, like butt cheeks or legs.

Read for filth
To criticise extremely harshly.

Realness

Serving realness has its origins from ballroom.
In a 'realness' category contestants have to show their
capability to pass and to blend into the real world.

Relying on body

A phrase used for drag queens that look very feminine
and have a good body, but no talent to speak of.

Sashay away

A goodbye phrase used by RuPaul when he is
eliminating a queen who has lost the lip-sync battle.

Shantay, you stay

Another phrase said by RuPaul, this time to the winner
of the lip-sync battle who will stay in the competition.

Snatched

A word describing perfection, especially used for wigs
and body shape.

Strut

To walk down a runway straight away with attitude.

Trade

A term for a sexually attractive guy who is available
for sex with a drag queen. The early meaning referred
to a straight, bicurious man having sex with a gay man,
trading sex for money, drugs or other services.

The Illustrator & the Author

Alba De Zanet is the illustrator of this book and lives in Bern, Switzerland. She loves colours and forms – the more diverse and cheekier, the better. Luckily, her style fits perfectly with the world of drag queens, a topic that she's totally in love with.

Roberto Garcia is the writer of this book and lives in the nice town of Winterthur, Switzerland. He loves binge-watching shows, especially series like *Will & Grace* and *RuPaul's Drag Race,* which is how he first became absorbed into the world of drag queens. The energy spreading from this subculture has also cast a spell over him in real life. He has become a walking drag queen dictionary, knows all the big names and is actively involved in the queer community.

Thank you so much!

A lot of the terms in this book and the vocabulary that drag queens, kings and drag enthusiasts are fiercely using nowadays **originated from the ballroom culture and from queer and trans people of colour.**

Ballroom culture not only created a new language, but also gave us new trends in fashion, dance styles, music and so much more.

We created this book to introduce people to the stunning world of drag culture and its vocabulary as well as pay tribute and give credit to ballroom culture and to the black queer and trans community.

Thank you for being such a great inspiration!

Disclaimer

Just have fun with it!

This book is meant to give a fun insight into the world of drag and the language that drag performers use daily.

The authors wanted to create a little handbook to introduce first-time drag audiences to the language, or to be a keepsake for drag superfans!

This list of terms and expressions is just a starting point to better understand drag lingo; the descriptions in this book are just a few of the many ways that the terms can be explained.

This book focuses on American drag culture; however, drag has different backgrounds around the world. Its vocabulary extends beyond English-speaking countries, and the language of drag is constantly evolving.

Imprint

Published in 2021 by Hardie Grant Books,
an imprint of Hardie Grant Publishing

Hardie Grant Books (London)
5th & 6th Floors
52–54 Southwark Street
London SE1 1UN

Hardie Grant Books (Melbourne)
Building 1, 658 Church Street
Richmond, Victoria 3121

hardiegrantbooks.com

British Library Cataloguing-in-Publication Data. A catalogue record for this book is
available from the British Library.

Drag Dictionary
ISBN: 978-1-78488-425-3
10 9 8 7 6 5 4 3 2 1

Publishing Director: Kate Pollard
Editor: Eila Purvis
Designer and illustrator: Alba De Zanet
Production Controller: Sinead Hering

Colour reproduction by p2d
Printed and bound in China by Leo Paper Products Ltd.

MIX
Paper from
responsible sources
FSC® C020056
FSC
www.fsc.org